Classical Themes
FOR FINGERSTYLE UKULELE
15 Solo Arrangements in Standard Notation & Tab

Arrangements by Pete Billmann

ISBN 978-1-4803-9150-5

HAL•LEONARD®
CORPORATION

7777 W. BLUEMOUND RD. P.O. BOX 13819 MILWAUKEE, WI 53213

In Australia Contact:
Hal Leonard Australia Pty. Ltd.
4 Lentara Court
Cheltenham, Victoria, 3192 Australia
Email: ausadmin@halleonard.com.au

Visit Hal Leonard Online at
www.halleonard.com

Ave Maria

By Franz Schubert

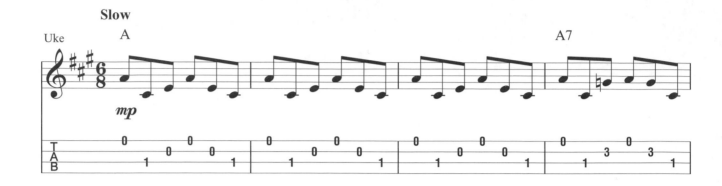

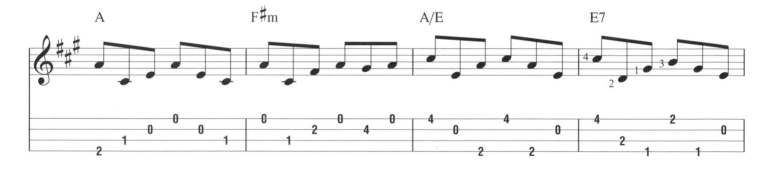

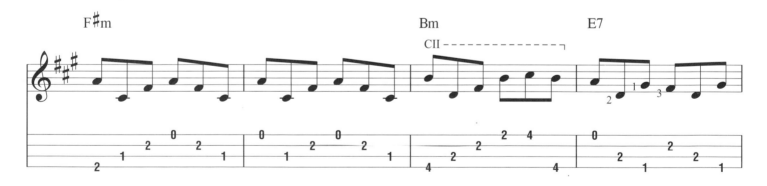

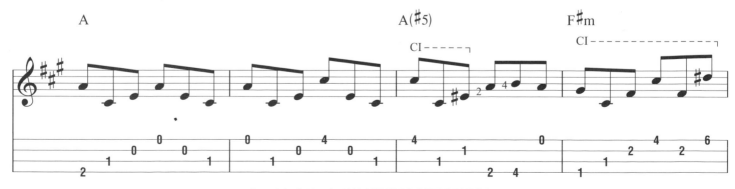

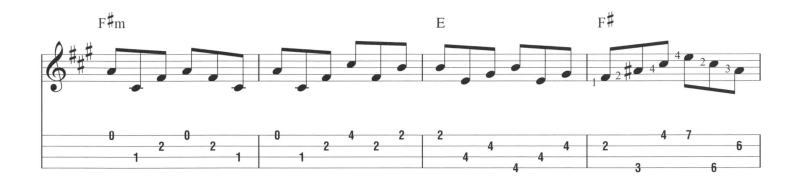

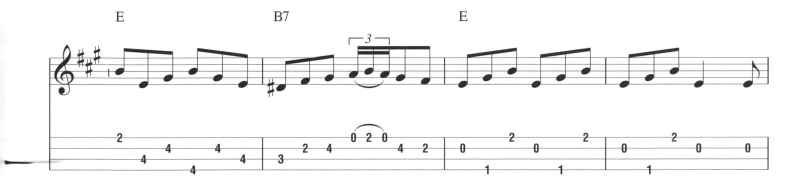

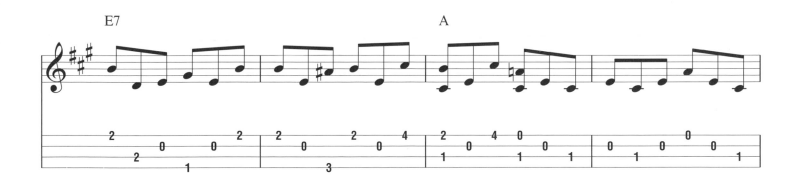

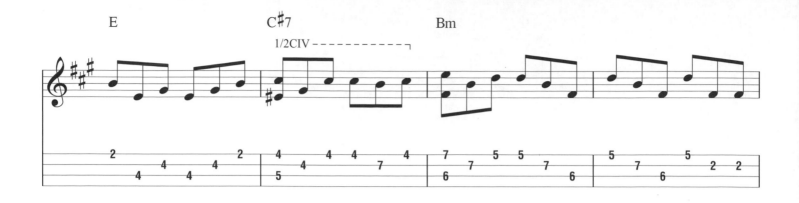

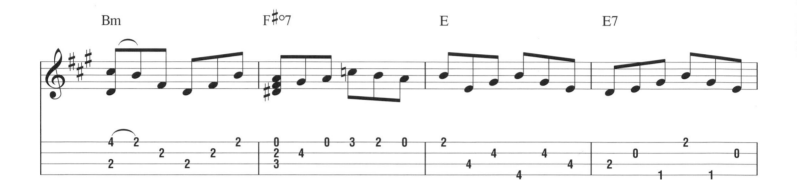

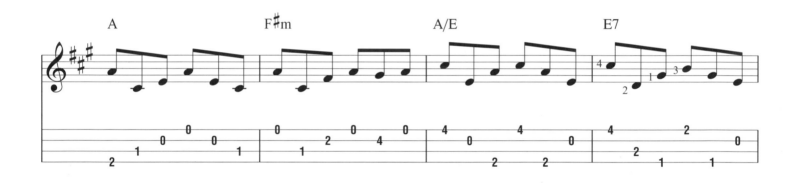

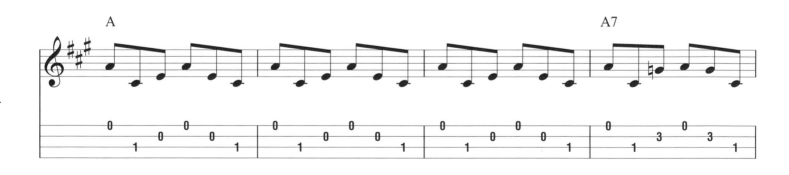

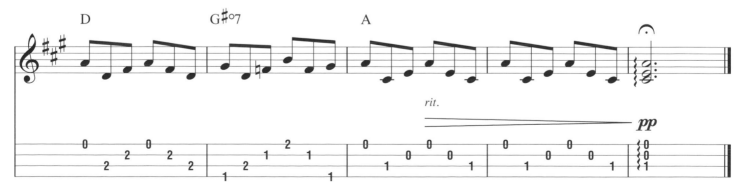

Eine Kleine Nachtmusik

("Serenade"), First Movement Excerpt

By Wolfgang Amadeus Mozart

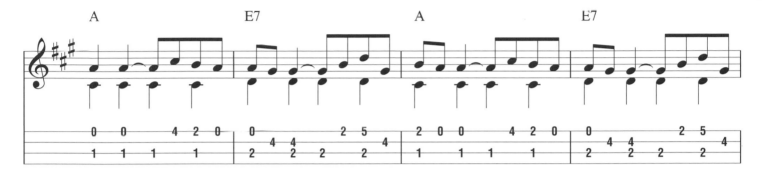

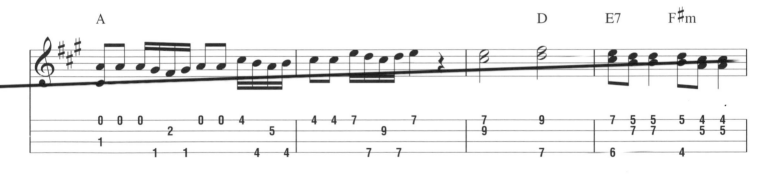

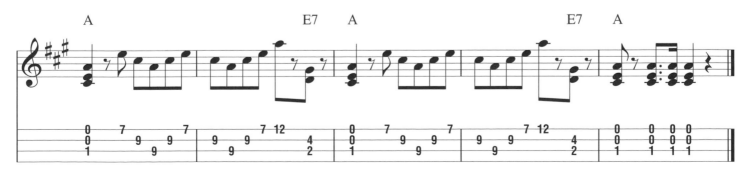

Blue Danube Waltz

By Johann Strauss, Jr.

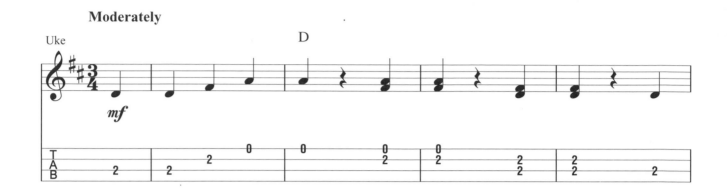

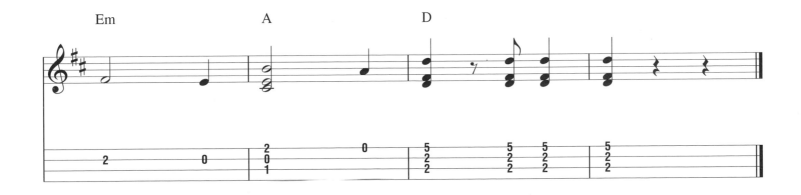

Canon in D

By Johann Pachelbel

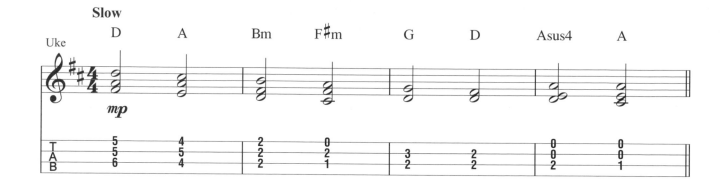

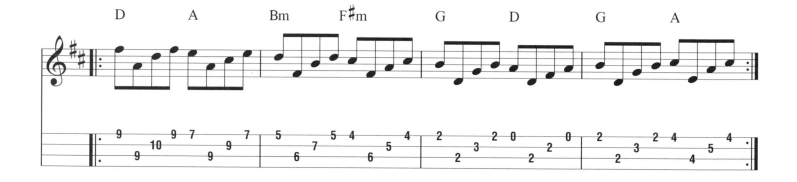

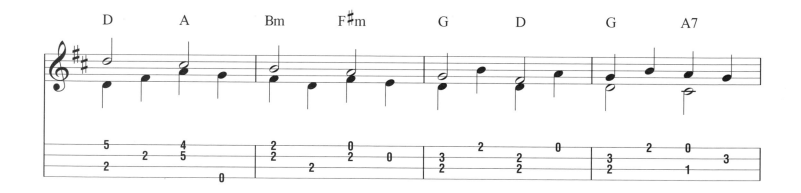

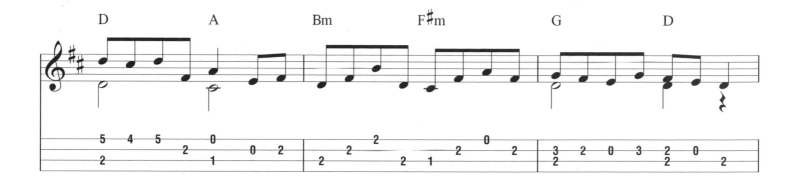

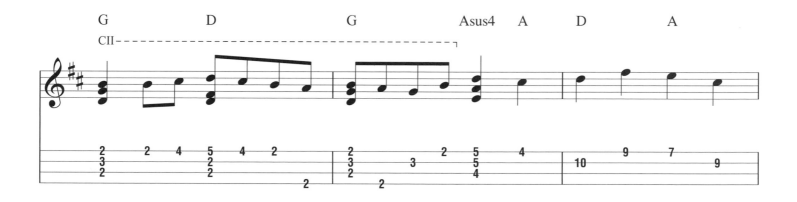

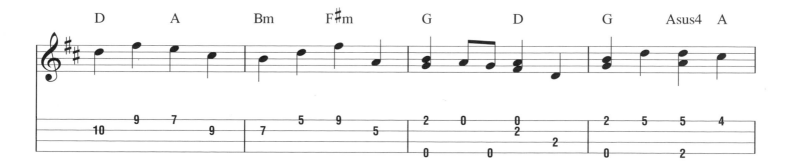

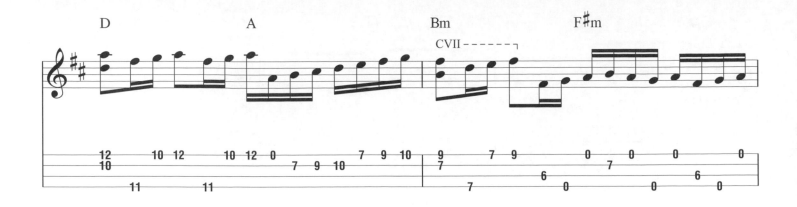

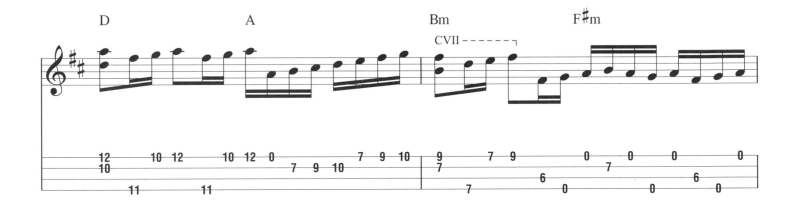

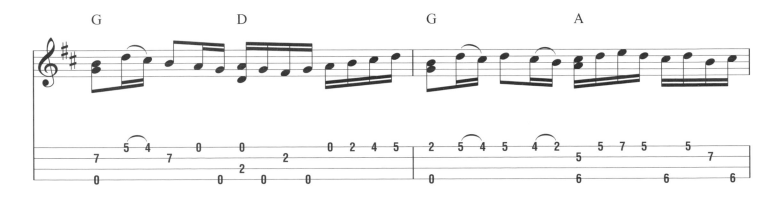

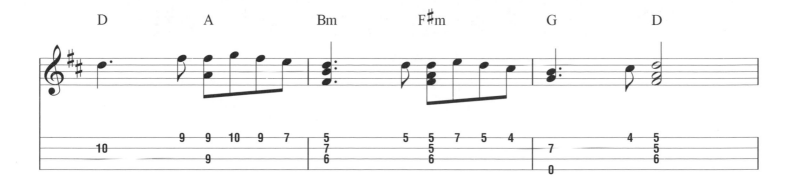

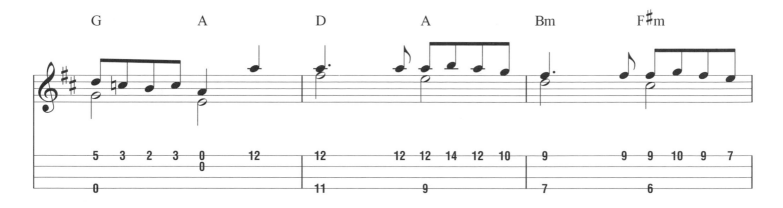

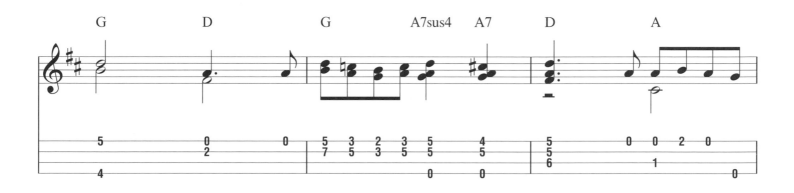

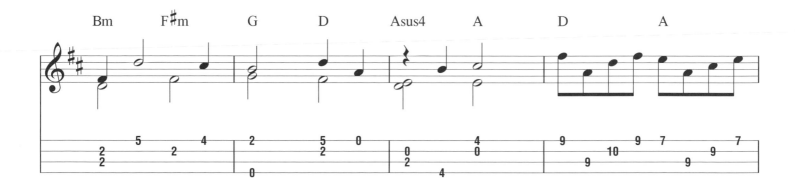

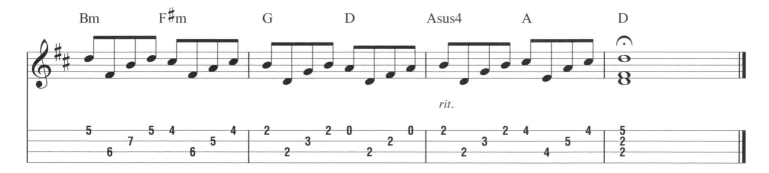

Funeral March of a Marionette

By Charles Gounod

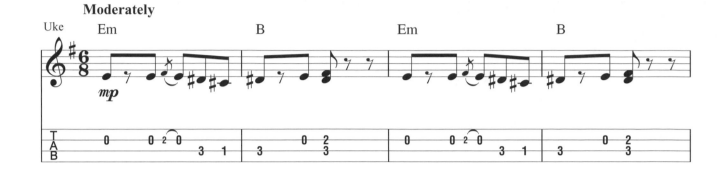

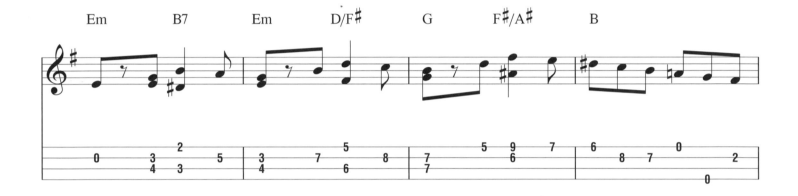

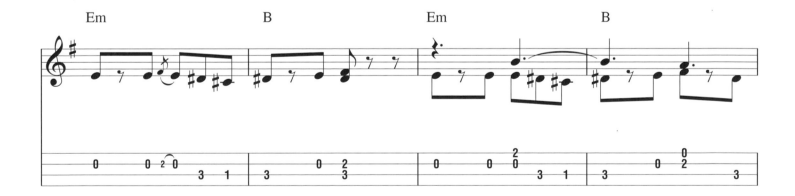

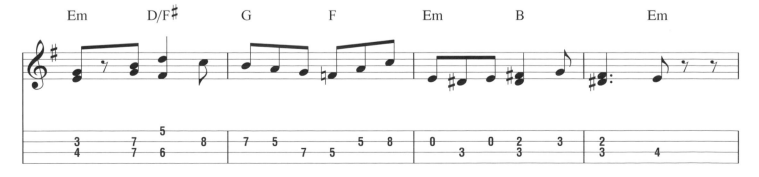

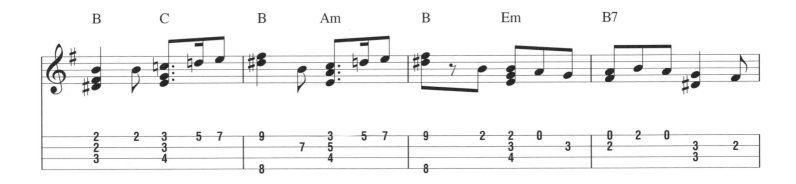

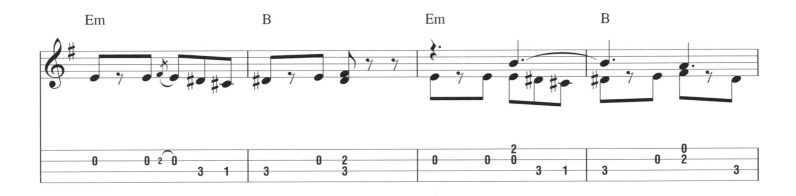

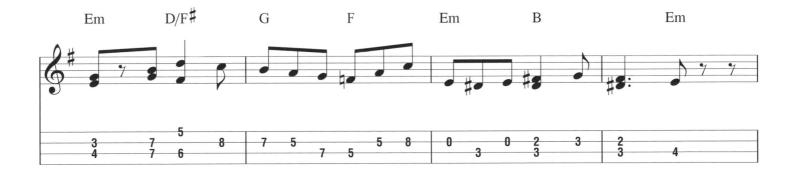

Für Elise

By Ludwig van Beethoven

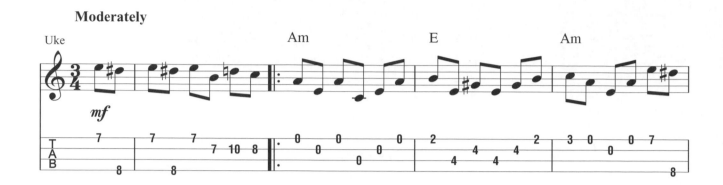

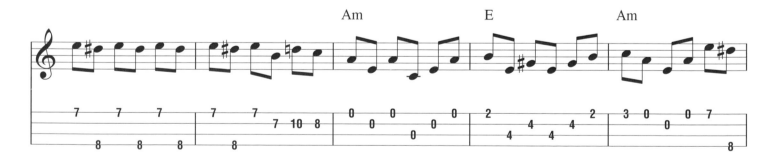

In the Hall of the Mountain King

from PEER GYNT

By Edvard Grieg

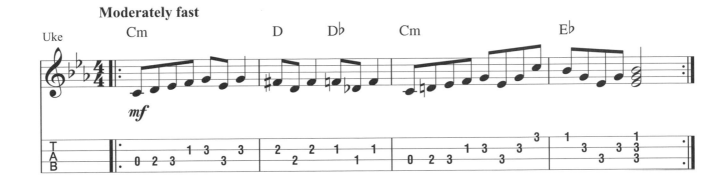

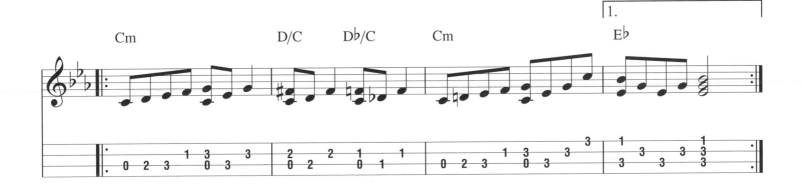

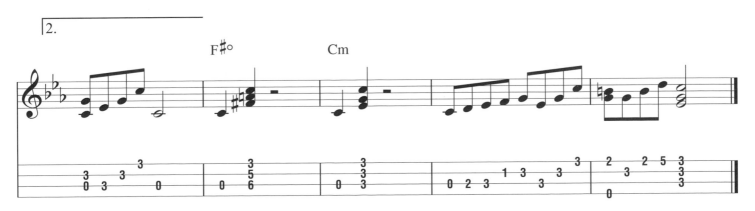

Habanera

from CARMEN

By Georges Bizet

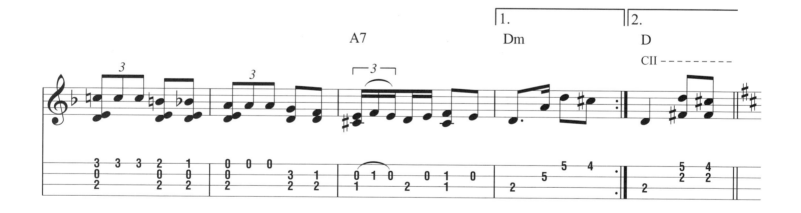

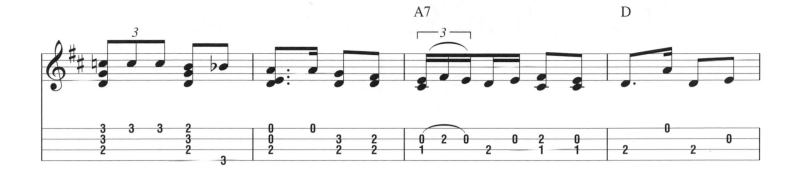

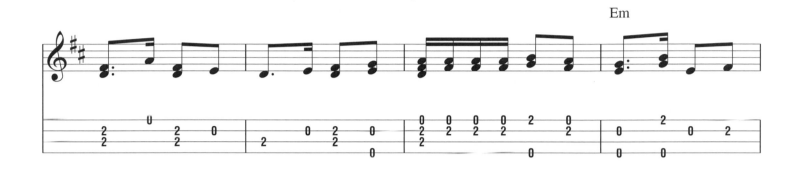

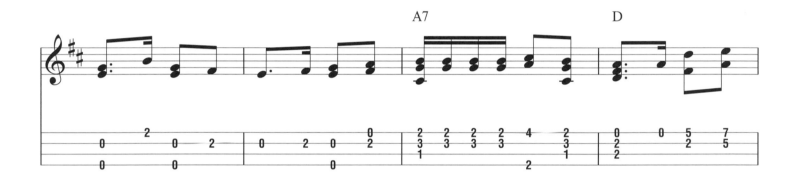

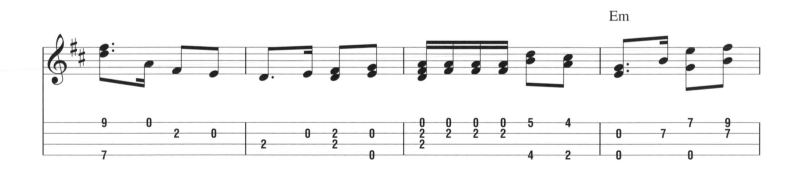

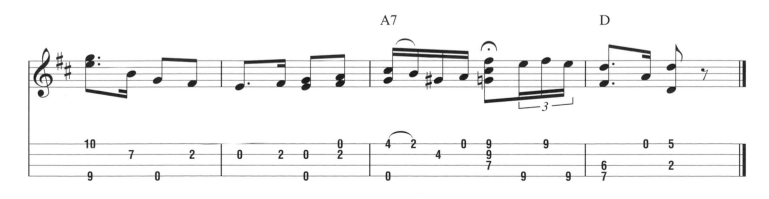

Largo from Symphony No. 9

("New World")

By Antonin Dvorak

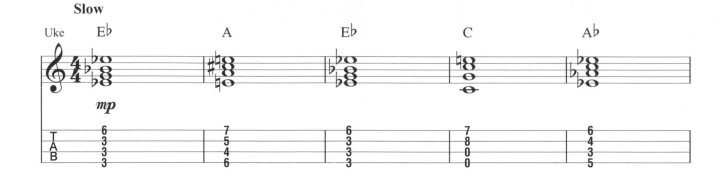

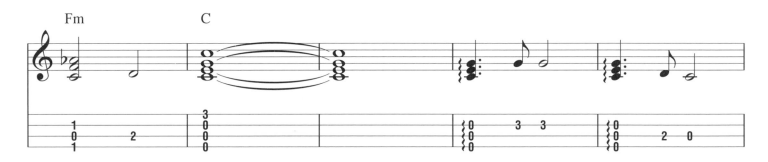

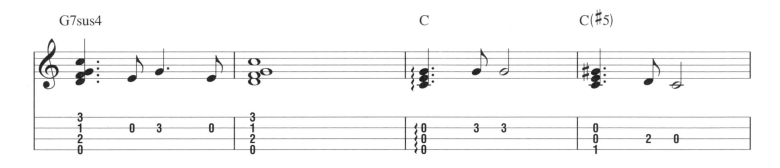

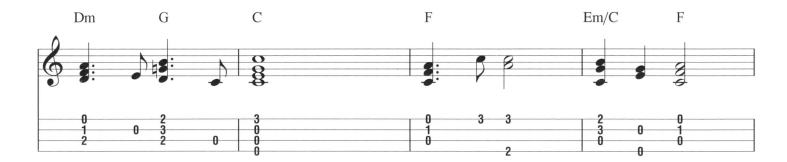

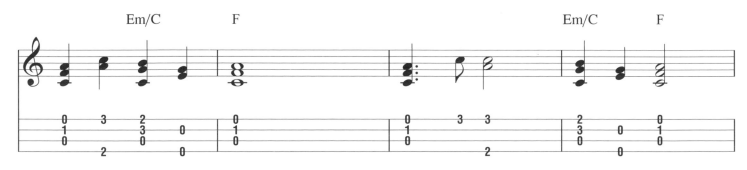

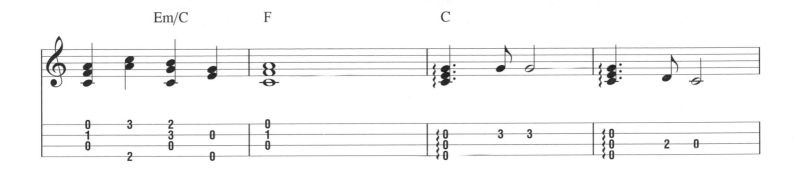

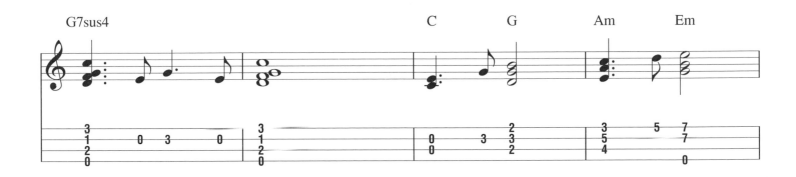

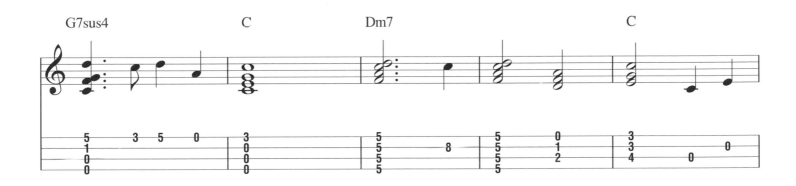

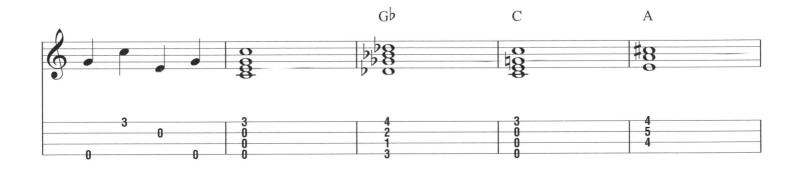

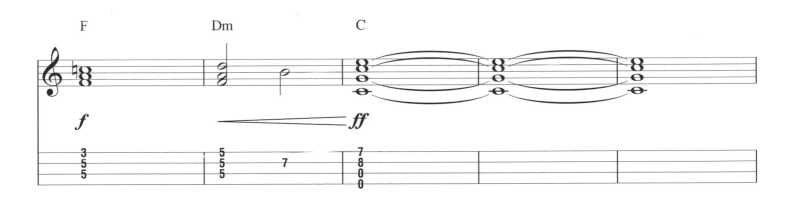

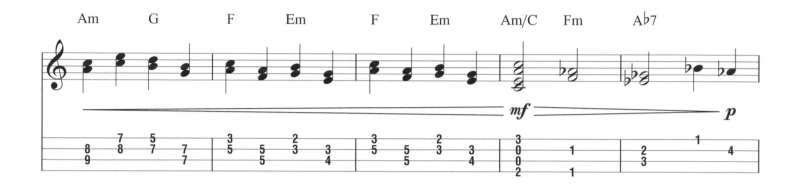

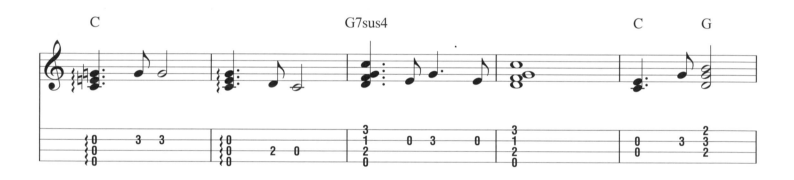

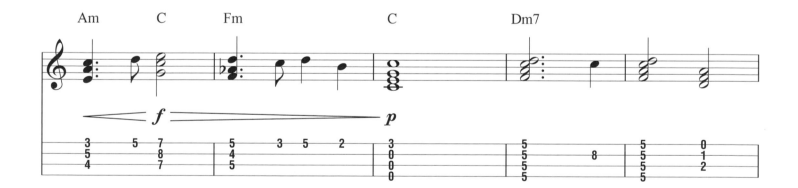

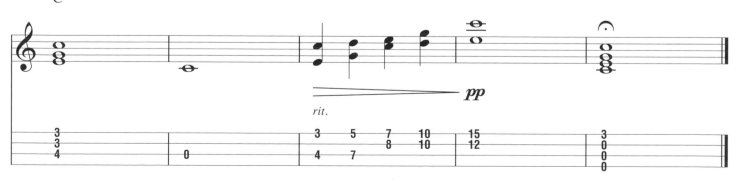

Piano Sonata No. 14 in C♯ Minor
("Moonlight") Op. 27 No. 2 First Movement Theme
By Ludwig van Beethoven

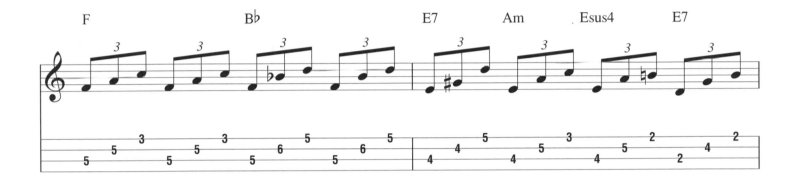

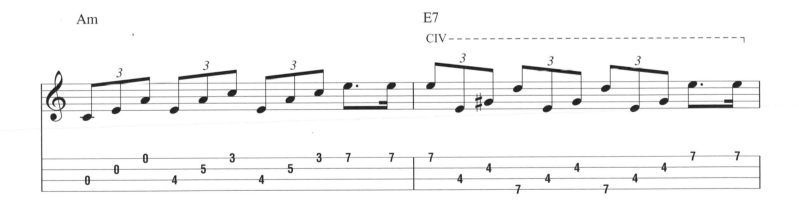

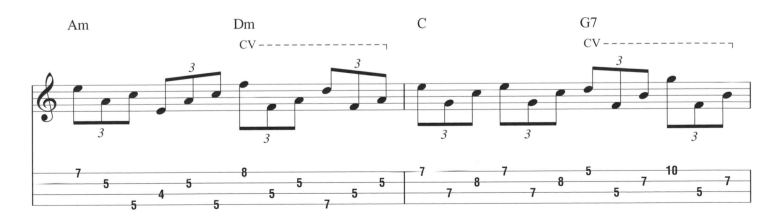

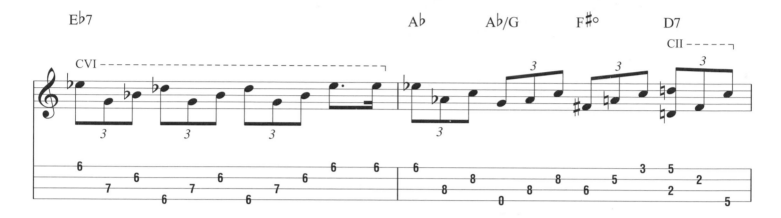

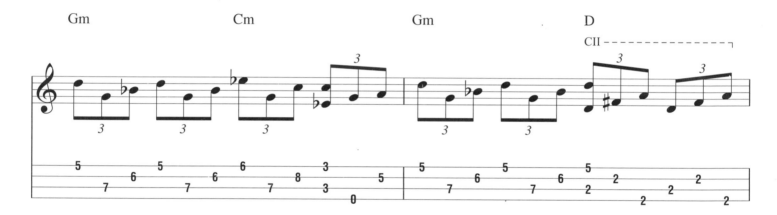

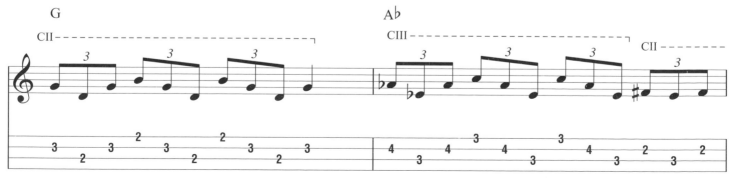

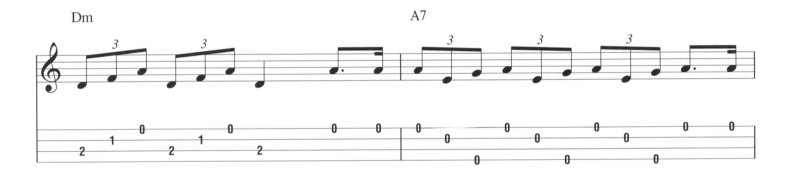

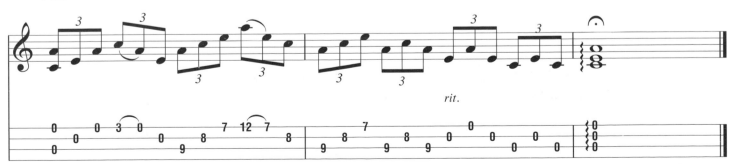

Morning

from PEER GYNT

By Edvard Grieg

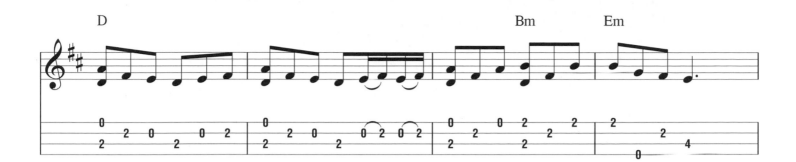

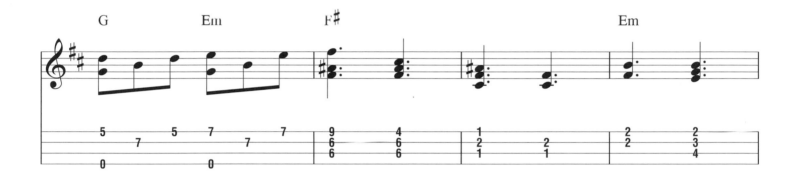

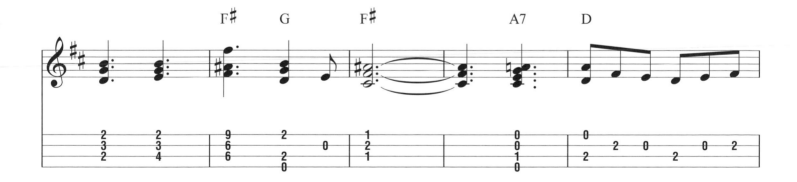

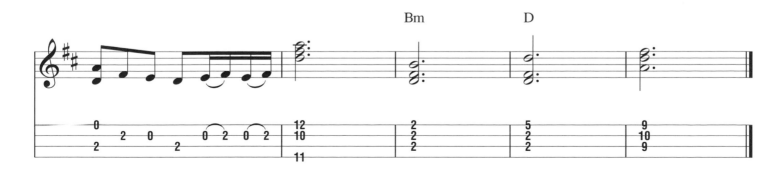

Rondeau

By Jean-Joseph Mouret

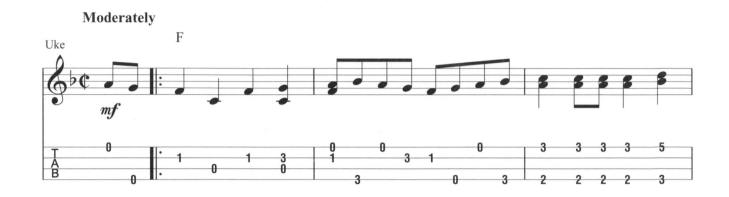

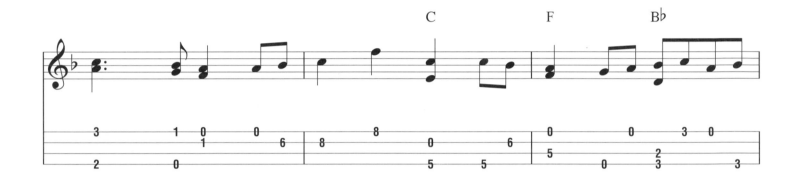

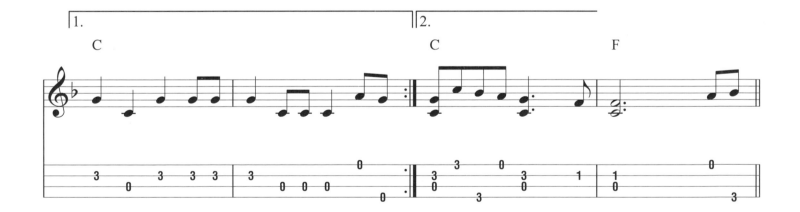

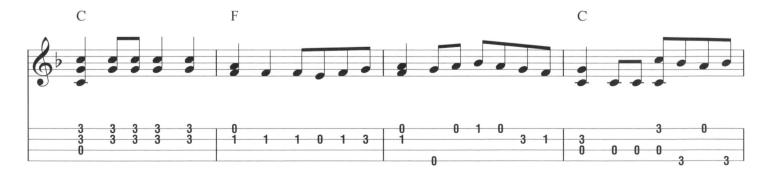

The Skaters (Waltz)

By Emil Waldteufel

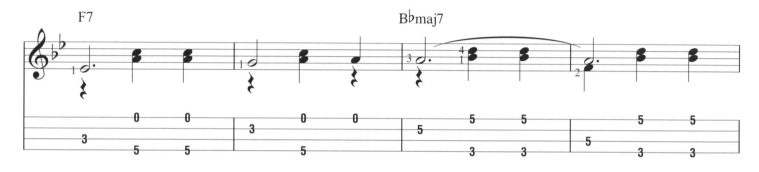

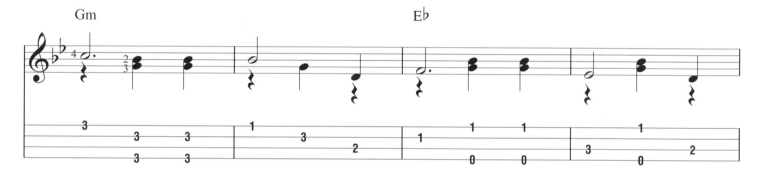

1.

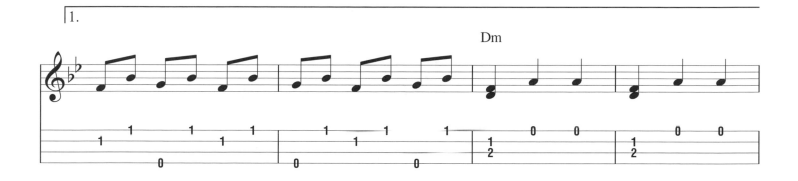

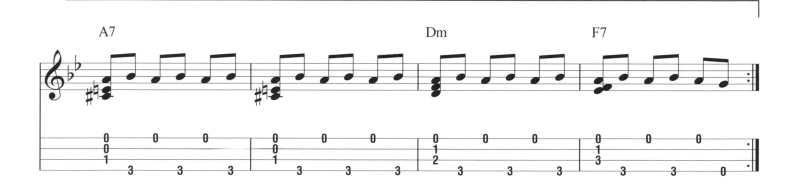

2.

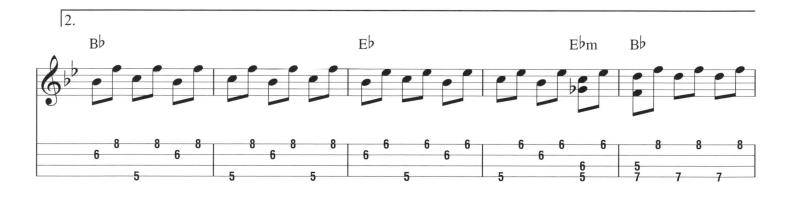

D.C. al Coda

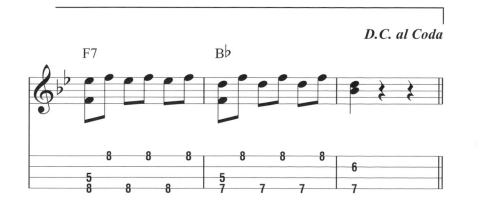

$\oplus$ **Coda**

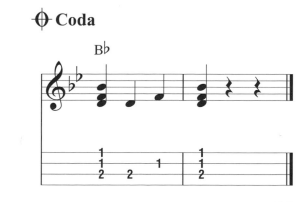

Spring

from THE FOUR SEASONS

By Antonio Vivaldi

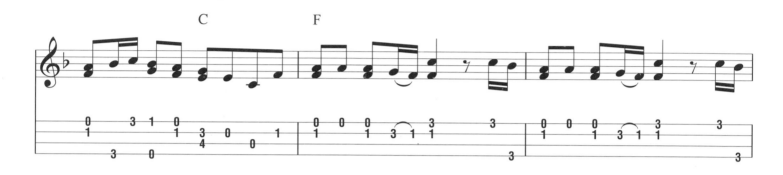

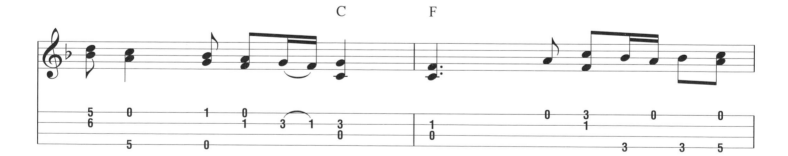

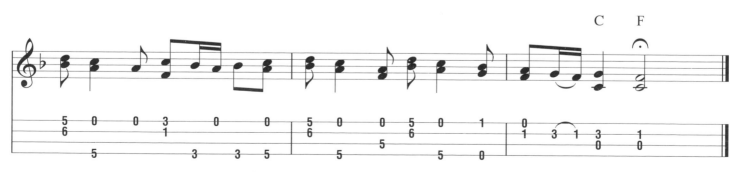

The Wild Horseman
Op. 68, No. 8
from ALBUM FUR DIE JUGEND (ALBUM FOR THE YOUNG)
By Robert Schumann

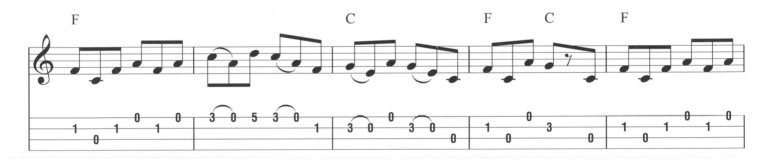

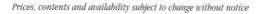